SONGS FROM THE FATHER

PAIGE SQUIRRELL

KINGDOM BREAKTHROUGH
Ministries

Do not be afraid. Do not let your hands fall limp. The Lord your God is in your midst, a warrior who saves. He will rejoice over you with joy; He will be quiet in His love [making no mention of your past sins], He will rejoice over you with shouts of joy.

— *ZEPHANIAH 3:16-17 (AMP)*

CONTENTS

INTRODUCTION

IS A LIFE OF JOY POSSIBLE?

Is it possible to live a life of joy? Paul says,

Always be full of joy in the Lord. I say it again - rejoice!

— *PHILIPPIANS 4:4 NLT*

Does God really expect us to always rejoice? What about those times we don't feel like it? What about when we experience one hardship after another and life isn't going the way we had hoped? Can we still be full of joy then? Is it even doable?

Paul tells us in Galatians that the Holy Spirit produces fruit in our lives. One part of this incredible fruit is 'Joy'. It is one of the keys God gives us to overcome and thrive, a key to seeing His Kingdom come and Heaven touch earth.

For the Kingdom of God is not a matter of what we eat or drink, but of living a life of goodness and peace and joy in the Holy Spirit.

— *ROMANS 14:17 NLT*

Our God is a God of joy. If we are to authentically reflect the heart of our Father, then joy needs to be woven into the very fabric of who we are. Being 'one' with our Father starts this beautiful weaving process.

Joy roots us. It changes our perspective on life, keeps hope alive, and encourages us to keep going when we would otherwise give up.

> *I pray that God, the source of hope, will fill you completely with joy and peace because you trust in him. Then you will overflow with confident hope through the power of the Holy Spirit.*
>
> *— ROMANS 15:13 NLT*

Paul commands us over and over again to 'rejoice in the Lord'. Nehemiah reminds us that 'the joy of the Lord is our strength'. David experienced the fullness of God's joy in the beauty of His Lord's presence. Apart from God, there isn't true, authentic, and genuine joy. If we are going to experience joy, we need to know God.

> *Be still and know that I am God.*
>
> *— PSALM 46:10 NLT*

True, authentic, real, and lasting joy can only come when we learn to drink deeply from the well of salvation. Those living waters satisfy, heal, encourage, inspire, and quench the thirst of pain, disappointments, dissatisfactions, disillusionments, and frustrations. No person or situation can rob us of those waters, unless they have our permission. As we drink, strength rises, perspectives change, hope increases, and life becomes possible.

Honour and majesty surround him; strength and joy fill his dwelling.

— 1 CHRONICLES 16:27 NLT

Joy filled the temple. Paul tells us in 1 Corinthians that we are the temple of the Holy Spirit. The Spirit of the living God is alive in us. He dwells in us. Joy is part of who God is. If He is alive in us, then we are carriers of joy, His complete joy. This is who we are. We are carriers of the joy of the Lord.

Take a moment and stop where you are. Thank your Father that you carry His Spirit and that His joy is alive in you. Smile. Imagine His joy bubbling up in you like a fountain ready to burst forth.

One of the greatest gifts God has given us is the gift of choice. It's tempting to think that if we don't feel something, then we aren't really experiencing it. The opposite is actually true. First we choose it, whether we feel it or not, and then as we keep choosing it, our feelings catch up and it becomes a reality. If we wait around to feel joy, we will never experience the full joy that the Father has for us. Joy doesn't depend on our circumstances. It depends on a person – God the Father, Son, and Holy Spirit. We choose joy by choosing God in every situation. We choose joy by saying 'yes' to Him in everything we face. Every time we choose joy, it becomes a natural part of who we are. It becomes our strength. It becomes our companion. Isaiah talks about receiving a cloak or garment of praise for a cloak of sorrow.

He has sent me to bind up the broken-hearted, to proclaim freedom for the captives and release from darkness for the prisoners, to proclaim the year of the Lord's favour and the day of vengeance of our God, to comfort all who mourn, and provide for those who grieve, ... to bestow on them a crown of beauty instead of ashes, the oil of joy instead of mourning, and a garment of praise instead of despair.

— ISAIAH 61:2-3 NLT

To live a life of joy, we need to choose to take off the heavy cloak of sorrow, which hinders us from moving forward and put on the cloak of praise. Joy isn't something we have to work hard at getting. Joy is a person we run to and embrace. It is found in the very essence and nature of our God. It is in Him that we encounter true joy.

Joy comes from a deep-rooted confidence and contentment in God. Only then can we fully understand James when he said, "Count it all joy when you face many trials," and Paul who said, "We can rejoice, too, when we run into problems and trials". How do we do that? It may seem morbid to be told to rejoice in our trials. However, life is not just about us. It's about us becoming more like Christ and impacting those around us. True joy is found in a life that is willing to embrace and model that. Both Paul and James point out that when we are able to face problems and trials with our eyes fixed on God, we develop endurance, strength of character, and a confident hope of salvation, which never leads to disappointment. Not only do we benefit from rejoicing, but others profit, as well. Joy changes perspectives, shifts atmospheres, and opens the door for God to do His work.

Joy comes from being able to see the bigger picture and embracing God's picture for His people and the world in which we live. Joy is not about what I feel or think; it's about what I choose and how I live. Hebrews 12:2 reminds us that the only way we can run the race in life is by fixing our eyes on Jesus. He is the perfect example of someone who chose joy and applied it to His life. It was the joy set before Him that enabled Him to endure the greatest suffering of all - the cross. He could have run away but He didn't. He knew the benefits the cross would have for all of humanity and this gave Him joy. It's this kind of joy that keeps us anchored and persevering when things get rough.

The only way we will know true and lasting joy is by taking our eyes off of the things around us and putting them on Jesus. He is our champion who has gone before us, our hero. He is the one who initiates and perfects our faith. And if we let Him, He is the one who will sustain us to the end. When we find ourselves flagging and wanting to give up, we look to Jesus and remind ourselves of all that He embraced and endured. This, in the words of Eugene Petersen, will shoot adrenaline into our souls. Locking eyes with our Saviour is the injection of joy that keeps us going and the hope of a great reward.

David experienced this first hand and describes it in Psalm 23. Life for him was not always easy. Yet he knew where to run. He knew where to hide. He knew where to sit. He knew where to stand. He knew how to sing and how to rejoice, regardless of what was going on around him. He knew the art of being still and knowing that God was God. He knew his Good Shepherd and trusted that all his needs were met in that one beautiful relationship they shared. This is how he kept going with hope and joy.

One of the greatest enemies of joy is fear. Fear opens the door to insecurity, rules and regulations, unforgiveness, grudges, bitterness, arrogance, the need to control, to strive, and to manipulate. It is no wonder that Timothy wrote,

For God has not given us a spirit of fear and timidity, but of power, love, and self-discipline.

— *2 TIMOTHY 1:7 NLT*

Fear will try to weave its way into our lives on a daily basis. Often we are only moments away from embracing it and giving it permission to control our thoughts and actions. Before we know it, chaos and confusion take over and joy is lost. It takes power from God to say 'no' to fear. It takes letting Him love us so that we can love Him and others to say 'no' to fear. And it takes self-discipline to choose to say 'no' to fear. Saying 'no' opens the door to faith and a life of joy in the presence of our Good Shepherd.

A TABLE FOR TWO

David talks about the Lord preparing a table for him in the presence of his enemies. Our greatest enemy is fear. Imagine a table set up for two, you and the Good Shepherd. The table is beautifully prepared as only our Father could do. He, who created beauty for us to enjoy, lays a table where we can receive truth and life right in the midst of our enemies. Imagine a jug of water flavoured with lemon and mint. Next to it a loaf of crusty bread is displayed ready to eat and the best kind of fruit vibrant in colour and full of flavour. In the whirlwind of lies, unfulfilled dreams, strained and lost relationships, unpaid bills, ongoing illnesses, anger, confusion, misunderstandings, discouragement, questions, unbelief, frustration, unforgiveness, and relentless comparisons, there is a table ready for you. You are invited to 'come, eat and drink'. In the thick of the winds and waves, there is a place ready for you, where you can regain your perspective and equilibrium.

David said 'The Lord is my Shepherd. I have all that I need. I lack nothing.' Later Jesus said, 'I am the Good Shepherd.' In Jesus we have all that we need. He is our living water and the bread of life. At this table for two, we learn to drink from the fountain of life and to eat the bread of life. We learn that as we eat and drink from the truths of our Good Shepherd, we have more than enough to face any storm. We find the strength to laugh and rejoice in the face of adversity. We receive truth and promises that sustain and carry us. We create space where the enemy has no hold or power over us. We receive life from the one who is life and find we can bear good and deep-rooted fruit in the midst of chaos and confusion. This is fruit that will last for all eternity.

We are His treasure, His prized possession, created to stand in awe of who He is. We capture His heart (Song of Songs 4:9). Showered with love and acceptance He wants us to be consumed with Him so that we experience His joy.

For the Lord your God is living among you. He is a mighty Saviour. He will take delight in you with gladness. With his love he will calm all your fears. He will rejoice over you with joyful songs.

— ZEPHANIAH 3:17 NLT

Our Good Shepherd is singing over us today. He longs to hold our attention, so that we can tune into the songs He is singing. He invites us to listen to His songs of rejoicing. Songs of acceptance. Songs of love. Songs of delight. Songs of encouragement. Songs of hope.

Come to the table for two. It's laid out for you and your Good Shepherd. Let Him secure your heart with His words of life and truth. Let Him sing over you with gladness. Drink His living water and you will never thirst again. Eat of the bread of life and you will never go hungry again. Be still and know that your Good Shepherd is who He says He is. Nothing will change this. You will be refreshed, restored, reinvigorated, ready to give out without burning out.

Come and sit. Eat, drink, and be full of joy as you listen to the Father singing over you.

WHAT TO EXPECT THIS MONTH

Every time we choose joy, we display a little more of God's nature and power at work in our lives. In this month, you have the opportunity to choose joy day by day. In the first week, you are invited to live out who you are in God. For the rest of the month, let joy become a part of who you are. Each day, there will be a declaration and an application.

This booklet contains 31 songs that the Father is singing over you. Listen and be forever changed. Enjoy!

PART I
WHO YOU ARE IN GOD

YOU ARE LOVED - LIVE LOVED

"I am love. My very nature is to love. You can know the love I have for you and completely rely on it. My love is relentless. It has gone the extra mile for you. My love is unconditional. It doesn't depend on your behaviour or your response to me. My love is unstoppable. Nothing, absolutely nothing, can thwart or hold back my love for you. My love is perfect in every way. It doesn't manipulate or control. It gives you free choice. You have the freedom to choose my love or to reject it. My love sees your fears and remains unshaken. It has the power to drive out your fears. Trust my love. It is perfect. It won't harm you. It has your best interest at heart.

I saw you locked in your sin, distant from me, and it moved my heart. I couldn't look on your sin. I had to do something to take care of the very things that were separating you from me. I longed for relationship with you. I longed to restore the intimacy lost in the Garden of Eden. My love made a way. Because I loved you, I sent my Son to die for you. He took the weight of your sin, which condemns and disqualifies you and bore it for you. He was condemned for you. He was rejected for you. He was ridiculed for you. He became sin for you. He became shame for you. He became disqualified so that you could be qualified in my eyes again. He paid every requirement so that we can do life together again. My love calls you mine. You are my child. My love gives you all of me. I am yours. You are mine and I am yours. You are my beloved and I am yours.

As my child, I long for you to live loved. Living loved is living free from the fear of punishment and condemnation. Living loved is embracing that Jesus qualifies you to stand perfect in my presence. Living loved gives you the courage and boldness to enter my throne room and receive grace and mercy whenever you need it. Living loved is becoming my glory and walking with your head held high because you know who you are and whose you are.

Live loved and you will hear my voice and do what I say. You will love me and others well and your joy will be made complete."

You are loved - live loved!

DECLARATION

I am loved with an unconditional and everlasting love by God who created the Heavens and the earth. I am His beloved and He is mine.

ACTIVATION

Spend some time meditating on God's love for you. Ask Him to reveal His love to you. Write down what He says. Live it out today.

————

John 3:16; Romans 8:15-16; 1 John 3:1

DAY 2

YOU ARE CHOSEN - LIVE CHOSEN

"I am the one who created you. I formed you in your mother's womb. You are hand knitted by me and I am proud of my creation. I flung the stars into space and breathed life into being. Come close, my chosen one, and receive the kiss of life. I have chosen you and brought you out of darkness into a spacious place of my wonderful light. There was a time when you didn't know who you were. This is no longer the case.

Your identity is secure in me because I have chosen you. You belong to me. You are my treasured possession. I chose you in advance and you can trust me to work everything out in your life according to the plans that I have written down for you. I don't choose like the world does. The world looks at outward appearances, abilities, successes and often holds every failure against you. It keeps a record of all the wrongs and defeat. I don't. I look at your heart. It's your heart that matters to me. If your heart is right, then the way you live today will be right. Everything you do and say indicates how healthy your heart is. I can do so much with one surrendered heart. A thankful heart for being chosen and a willing heart to serve is all I need to see my purposes fulfilled in and through your life. Your 'yes' to me opens the door for me to do a work in you.

When I chose you, it was intentional. I chose you before you were born because I knew you would be the best 'you'. Society will try to get you to be someone or something else. But I created you to be 'you'. With my help, you can become the best 'you' there is. Stop comparing yourself to others. I haven't called you to be like them. I have called you to be who I have made you to be. I will equip you and give you everything you need each step of the way. So don't be afraid. Trust me and live chosen. I will never fail you. Live chosen and you will choose well.

Acknowledge me as your Creator, the one who gives your life purpose, the one whose thoughts and ways are much higher than yours, and you will go from strength to strength. I relieve you from the stress of having to do life on your own and in your own strength. I offer you all my resources so that you can choose life and live well. Receive and live as my chosen one.

Live chosen and you will stay alert. You will be able to discern and watch out for the lies of the enemy. You will stand firm against him because you know who you are in me. You will become strong in your faith. Your joy will be made complete, my chosen one."

You are chosen - live chosen

DECLARATION

I am my Father's treasured possession, chosen to do life in partnership with Him.

ACTIVATION

How does the truth that you are the Father's treasured possession change the way you will live today?

———

Ephesians 1:11; Colossians 3:12; 1 Peter 2:9-10; 5:8-9; 4:19

DAY 3

YOU ARE ACCEPTED - LIVE ACCEPTED

"I sent my Son, Jesus, to reveal my heart to the world I created. He came to reveal my heart to you. Those who have seen my Son have seen me. Those who know my Son, know me. The Spirit I have given you doesn't cause you to panic and live in fear. It's not a 'spirit of religious duty', constantly striving and never feeling good enough. No, how can you live like that?

The Spirit you have received from me is the 'Spirit of full acceptance'. I accept you. You are mine. I am your Father. There's nothing you can do to not be accepted and there's nothing more you have to do to be accepted. My Son did it all. When He cried 'It is finished!', He declared His sufficiency to every person watching on the day, and to everyone who would look to the cross in the future. His work at the cross is sufficient for you. It is enough. It released my Spirit of acceptance to a world I couldn't look at because of sin.

Remember, I had to turn away from my Son. I couldn't look at Him when He bore all your sin. He has taken it all. You no longer need to live under the burden of it. The curse of sin has been broken in your life.

There is only one God, me, your Father. I have created all things. I am the source of all things. I am your source.

There is only one Lord, Jesus, my Son, the Anointed one, through whom you and everything else exists. Nothing else matters.

When you embrace this truth, all your worries and anxieties will be replaced with a reason for being; a reason to live accepted. Live accepted and you will be focused on me and my best for your life. Live accepted and my protection and security will be yours. Live accepted and you will walk in victory. Live accepted and you will hear the songs I sing over you as your good, good Father. Your joy will be complete."

You are accepted - live accepted!

DECLARATION

I am accepted by my Father, not because of what I do but because of who I am. I am His beloved child.

ACTIVATION

Write down three truths about your relationship with your good, good Father and meditate on them throughout the day.

———

Psalm 32:7; Romans 8:15; 15:6; 1 Corinthians 8:6

DAY 4

YOU ARE FAVOURED - LIVE FAVOURED

"You are my favoured one. I know you by name and I look on you with eyes of favour. My favour is my gift to you. You have it for a lifetime. My favour isn't something I give and then take away again. It's there for you every day of your life. You don't deserve it and you will never be able to earn it so don't even try. Favour comes when you accept my Son, Jesus, as your Lord and Saviour. My favour is your protection. It's a shield. It's a covering of kindness and joy.

When lies, hard times, frustrations, false accusations, and disappointments attack your peace and try to knock you off course, seek shelter under the canopy of my favour. There you'll find your equilibrium again. It's a joy and delight to pour out my favour and honour on your life. I am your generous Father. I love to provide. I won't withhold anything that is good from you. I want my favour to rest on you so that I can establish the works of your hands and give you success in everything you do. Look to me and walk in my ways.

My Son grew in favour with me and with man. Learn to do the same. Favour sets you apart. Favour moves you forward. Favour positions you for my rewards. Believe the words that I speak are true and confidently trust that I am who I say I am and that I will do what I say I will do, and the favour on your life will increase.

Today is the day to respond to my favour. Today is the day of salvation. My favour will keep you going when the going gets tough. It will keep you alert, unmoved with a pure heart and clear head. You will be full of love and gentleness as you live the life I have called you to live. My favour will enable you to bring glory to my name so that your joy will be complete."

You are favoured - live favoured!

DECLARATION

God's grace/favour gives me strength. His divine influence on my life enables and empowers me. I can live today because He gives me strength.

ACTIVATION

Thank God for His favour on your life. Be aware of His grace/favour today and talk about it unashamedly. Give Him glory.

———

Psalm 5:12; 30:5; 84:11; 90:17; Luke 2:52; 2 Corinthians 6:2; Hebrews 13:9

YOU ARE SECURE - LIVE SECURE

"Remember, you are my beloved. As my beloved, you can rest in me and be secure. I am the one who shields you all day long. You can rest in me and find the security you need today. Society will offer you all kinds of things that promise you security. It will get you to strive for 'more' things that you can see and touch. My security is not in what you can see or touch. My security is rooted in a deep inner peace and joy that no one can take from you. Nothing can destroy it. No fire, no flood, no tragedy, no financial collapse, no death, no loss, nothing can steal your inner peace and joy unless you let it.

Don't be fooled into thinking that the things you can see and touch will make you strong and secure. I am the one who arms you with strength and keeps your way secure. I am the one who provides everything you need.

I am the source of your life and security. Without me, you will never know the meaning of secure living. I am your security; you will never be shaken. You are rooted in my love and you can stand strong and secure.

In my Son you have an anchor that will hold you firmly and securely in times of peace and in times of turmoil and distress.

Trust my security more than anything else that is on offer and you will live secure. Your joy will be complete."

You are secure - live secure!

DECLARATION

God is my hiding place and I am safe under the shadow of His wings. My security depends on Him, not on what others think and say, or how I am feeling.

ACTIVATION

Take time to shelter in your Father's presence. Read Psalm 91. Are there any feelings or thoughts that are causing insecurity? Hand them to the Father and allow Him to sing His truths over you. Write them down, dwell on them, and let them replace the lies.

———

Deuteronomy 33:12; 2 Samuel 22:33; Psalm 18:32; 30:6

DAY 6

YOU ARE ALIVE - LIVE ALIVE

"I am the living God. There is no one like me. I will endure forever. My kingdom will never be destroyed and my rule and reign will never end. I am alive and I am able to rescue and save my people from their sleep and slumber. I am able to perform miraculous signs and wonders in the heavens and on the earth. I am alive and my Son is alive.

The same Spirit that raised Jesus from the dead lives in you. If you are walking in relationship with me, then my spirit is alive in you. He is active in you. No fire or storm, defeat or setback, drought or flood can ever snuff the life out of you, because I am alive in you. Christ in you is your hope and glory. Christ in you is your lifeline. Christ in you is enough. You are alive in Him and He is alive in you.

So no matter what, you will live. No matter what, you can bear fruit. No matter what, you have the power to thrive because we are one. There's no excuse not to be fully alive every moment of every day. Daily, you have the privilege of experiencing life on my terms because we are one. I want to live and breathe in you today, causing you to come alive to my way of thinking and living. This is the resurrection life I have for you. This is life in all its fullness. Timidity and fear no longer control you. My resurrection life fills you with an expectation for adventure and all that I have for you. It confirms who you really are. You are mine and I am yours. You are alive in the good times and the hard times. I am always with you and will walk with you giving you life each step of the way. My resurrection life makes your joy complete."

You are alive - live alive!

DECLARATION

I am alive in Christ. The same Spirit that raised Jesus from the dead lives in me. Nothing and no one can take that from me. Jesus is my glory and the lifter of my head, opening the door to a full and fruitful life.

ACTIVATION

Ask God to infuse everything you think, say, and do today with His resurrection life. Breathe in that life. Believe that you will produce fruit today because His Spirit is alive in you.

———

Jeremiah 17:7-10; Daniel 6:26-27; Romans 8:9-20

DAY 7

YOU ARE FREE - LIVE FREE

"I have called you to a life of freedom. It hurts to see my children walk around bound up with chains that are cripple them and hold them back from everything I intended for them before the beginning of time. You can only walk in the freedom I have for you, if you receive my grace. This grace enables and empowers you to do what is right. My grace keeps you going when life seems impossible. My grace sustains and strengthens you so that your natural desires no longer control you. My desires become your desires. My thoughts and words become your thoughts and words. This is the freedom I have for you.

Before the beginning of time, it was my plan to show you my grace through Jesus Christ. This grace was not so that you have freedom to live for yourself. Living for yourself will only destroy the freedom you have in me. Grace, fully received and embraced, leads to awe and wonder of what I have done and continue to do in your life. Remember, I will always finish what I have started in the lives of my children. It is so much easier when my children learn to co-operate with me. Grace gives you the freedom to love me with all your heart, soul, and mind, and to love others as I have loved you.

You can't do this when you are consumed with yourself. Be

completely consumed with me and you will experience freedom. Receive grace and love and walk in the freedom I have for you. Then give away the grace and love you have received and experience an increase in freedom. In the natural, you give away and you end up with less. In my Kingdom, you give away and you end up with more because I honour and replenish what you have given. Try it, you will be surprised and it will become a way of life. I am a God of freedom. I haven't created you to be a slave chained to yourself and your circumstances. In Jesus Christ, you are free. It is up to you to stay free. I can't do that for you. I have already made freedom possible, now it's up to you to embrace it.

Allow the truth of my words to get hold of your heart so that it beats with the same heartbeat that mine does. Just like food nourishes your body and keeps you physically healthy, my words nourish your spirit and bring freedom. Listen to my words. Read them. Meditate on them. Wash yourself in them. Freedom will be yours without an ounce of strife and your joy will be complete."

You are free - Live free!

DECLARATION

It is for freedom that Christ has set me free. I stand firm in that freedom and refuse to go back into the bondage of my past.

ACTIVATION

Ask the Father if there are any areas where you are not walking in the freedom Jesus bought for you. Is there anyone you need to forgive? Do you need to forgive yourself? Forgive. Surrender to His Spirit today and let Him produce His fruit of freedom in your life.

————

Matthew 4:4; Galatians 1:4; 5:1, 13; Ephesians 5:26; 2 Timothy 1:9

PART II
LIVING A LIFE OF JOY

DAY 8

Be joyful at your festival - you, your sons and daughters, your male and female servants, and the Levites, the foreigners, the fatherless and the widows who live in your towns. For seven days celebrate the festival to the Lord your God at the place the Lord will choose. For the Lord your God will bless you in all your harvest and in all the work of your hands, and your joy will be complete.

— DEUTERONOMY 16:14-15

"I am the one who blesses you. I am the one who gives you success. Never lose sight that every blessing and every success has its source in me. I am the one who gives you the desire and the power to do what pleases me. I am the one who makes your path straight and leads you forward step by step. My heart for you is that you would learn to celebrate these things in your life and not take them for granted. I give you all things to enjoy. As you learn to rejoice moment by moment, your eyes will be opened to the way I work. You will become more intentional in the way you live life.

Learn to celebrate. Let celebration become a part of your

daily routine and who you are. It's an art that takes practice and one that captures my heart and brings me delight. It may not come naturally to you but the more you do it, the easier you will find it. So celebrate. And then, when you have finished celebrating, celebrate again. Look for new things to celebrate. Look for new ways to celebrate and your joy will become complete and infectious."

DECLARATION

I bring my Father pleasure every time I choose to rejoice. The Lord has made me strong. My heart rejoices.

ACTIVATION

Choose one thing to celebrate today and share it with someone. Declare how great God is and what He has done for you. Make a big thing about Him to your family and friends. Don't be shy. Don't feel stupid. Celebrate the goodness of your Father.

———

1 Samuel 2:1-2; Philippians 2:13; 1 Timothy 6:17

DAY 9

For great is the Lord and most worthy of praise; he is to be feared above all gods. For all the gods of the nations are idols, but the Lord made the heavens. Splendour and majesty are before him; strength and joy are in his dwelling place.

— 1 CHRONICLES 16:25-27

"You are my dwelling place; the temple of my Holy Spirit. You carry my strength and my joy because my Spirit lives in you. When you have a revelation that I am your great God, the God above all other gods, the God who is the almighty and powerful one, the God who was and is and is to come, you will tap into the strength and the joy that is already in you because I am in you. Make a joyful sound and you will move my heart and cause me to work on your behalf. My presence gives you an occasion to rejoice. Because I am always with you, you will never be without a reason to rejoice. Rejoice in me. Praise my name. Declare my greatness and watch my joy and strength become a greater part of your every day. With every decree and shout, your joy will become more complete."

DECLARATION

Great are you, Lord, and most worthy of praise. You are full of splendour and majesty. My strength is found in rejoicing in you.

ACTIVATION

Take a few minutes and sing out your own song. It doesn't matter what it sounds like. God looks at the heart from which it is sung. He just sang over you and He longs to hear your song of praise. You can start with something like, "Great are you, Lord, and most worthy of praise…"

———

1 Chronicles 15:16; Nehemiah 8:10

DAY 10

And on that day they offered great sacrifices, rejoicing because God had given them great joy. The women and children also rejoiced. The sound of rejoicing in Jerusalem could be heard far away.

— NEHEMIAH 12:43

"Your joy comes from one source and one source alone - me! I am your joy. Joy is my gift to you. Receive it. Walk in it. Let it saturate every thought you think, every word you speak, and every action you take. Looking in other places for your joy will only lead to disappointment. Look to me and you will never be put to shame. You will radiate me in my glory and joy. Learn to take a long drink from the fountain of salvation. Don't gulp. Take a moment and savour each sip of truth. Meditate on your incredible gift of salvation. Pause and give thanks that I am no longer angry with you. Celebrate that sin has been dealt with once and for all. Rejoice that the victory has been won. Shout for joy that you no longer have to try and satisfy me in your own strength. My Son paid the price that you could never pay. Exult that He became like you so that you could become like Him.

Jump for joy that I will always be with you and that I will never leave you on your own. Be on top of the world for all the wonderful things I have done for you. List them one by one.

Give thanks, rejoice, celebrate and then give thanks, rejoice, and celebrate again. Never stop giving thanks and rejoicing. Every sip of gratitude from the well of salvation will take away all fear and increase your trust and joy in me. Do a twirl. Jump up and down. Dance a jig. Release the sound of rejoicing and your joy will be complete."

DECLARATION

God is my source of joy. I have much to celebrate. My life releases the sound of rejoicing everywhere I go because I am filled with great joy.

ACTIVATION

Take a few moments and make a list of all the wonderful things Father God has done for you. Give thanks, rejoice, and celebrate in a new way. Do something you haven't done before or that you wouldn't normally do. (Stepping outside our comfort zone releases something supernatural.)

————

Isaiah 12

DAY 11

The precepts of the Lord are right, giving joy to the heart. The commands of the Lord are radiant, giving light to the eyes.

— PSALM 19:8

"I want to show you the way to joy. Listen to what I have to say. My precepts and commands are not to restrict you or to cause you grief. They are there to influence your thinking and your behaviour leading you to wholeness and joy. They are right. They are good. They are signposts to all I have for you. They may not line up with current thinking but remember my thoughts and ways are above current thoughts and ways.

If you desire pure, authentic joy, eyes full of light, seeing all that I have for you, then learn to say 'yes' to my precepts and commands. Follow my line of thinking. Follow my words. Follow my ways. You won't be disappointed. My words are more desirable than gold. They are sweeter than honey. Listen closely to my words. My words are always true. They will always achieve what is best for you. Chew on them. Digest them. Let them penetrate deep into your heart. Let them nourish your mind, body, soul, and spirit. They will bring you joy regardless of what life throws at you. The more you love my words and commands, the closer you will be to my heart. That is the place of complete joy."

DECLARATION

The instructions of my Father are right and they bring great joy to my heart. I will listen to His words and walk in His ways. He gives me insight for living.

ACTIVATION

Is there a situation where you need insight, instruction, or a strategy. Take a few moments and ask the Father to speak to you about it. Write it down. Put it into practice.

———

Psalm 19:9-10; Proverbs 4:10-13, 20-23; Isaiah 58:11

DAY 12

Around midnight Paul and Silas were praying and singing hymns to God.

— ACTS 16:25

"Tortured and bound in chains, Paul and Silas prayed and sang hymns to me. In my presence there is always fullness of joy. Chains, torture, darkness, frustration, broken dreams, unfulfilled hopes, sickness, poverty are never obstacles to my presence. My presence will always overcome. It is not limited to just the good times. I am always with you in the rough and the smooth, the good and the bad, the successes and the failures. Look for me in everything you face. Lock eyes with me. Fix your gaze on me and start to pray and sing. Prayer and singing break chains. They open prison doors. They release my presence and increase your joy. When you feel like it, pray and sing. When you don't feel like it, pray and sing.

Pray! Sing! And watch my joy expand to fill all the spaces in your life, even those that are hard to fill. My joy will fill you, transform you, and change the way you see your situation. My joy will be your strength and your song.

Pray! Sing! Ride the wave of my joy today and you won't get stuck or sink in the quagmire of life.

Pray! Sing! And your joy will be complete."

DECLARATION

No matter what today brings, I will find the energy to pray and sing. Nothing can rob me of my song of praise. Praise makes a way for God to work.

ACTIVATION

Is there a situation in which you are longing for breakthrough? Spend some time praising your Father. Praise in the midst of irritation produces character and beauty. It brings about God's best in our lives.

––––––

Psalm 16:8; Acts 16:16-40

DAY 13

The Lord will display his glory, the splendour of our God. …
those who cannot speak will sing for joy! … Sorrow and
mourning will disappear, and they will be filled with joy and
gladness.

— ISAIAH 35:2, 6, 10

"Be encouraged. Regardless of what you are facing, you will
see my glory displayed and my splendour revealed. Even in
your darkest hour, there is room for my glory to shine through
and radiate my goodness. Begin to sing. It may start out weak, a
mere whisper. But as you continue, your song will become a
shout. You will find your voice. Though it is faint because of
what you are experiencing, you will be able to sing.

Sing for joy! Be strong and do not fear! I am here to protect
you from the things that come against you and my purposes for
your life. You are not on your own. I am here to save you. Let me
open your eyes to what I am doing at this time. Let me open your
ears to my plans and ways. I want to see you thrive in life, not
just survive. The world will see my glory displayed in and
through you. My glory will fill the earth just like the waters cover

the sea. Nothing can come against my glory and prevent it from shining. I am your glory and I am the one who lifts your head. I, in you, display my glory through you.

Come to me today and let me lift your head so that you can sing. Sing for joy! Every song you sing while walking through dry, dark, and hard times is another opportunity for my glory to be displayed in and through you. Every choice to focus on me and my ways rather than on your circumstances, is an opening for my joy to be made complete in you."

DECLARATION

I will rise and sing. The Lord is my glory and the lifter of my head. I can smile at the future because my Father's hand is on my life and His purposes will prevail. His glory will be displayed for all to see.

ACTIVATION

Stand up. Smile and sing to the Lord until you can feel joy welling up inside you and any darkness lift.

―――――

Psalm 3:3; 72:19; Proverbs 31:25

DAY 14

For seven days they celebrated with joy the Festival of Unleavened Bread, because the Lord had filled them with joy...

— EZRA 6:22

"I am your source of authentic joy. I am the one who fills you with joy. Looking for joy anywhere, other than in me, will inevitably lead to disappointment at some time in your life. Welcome me as your source of joy and you will never be disappointed. One look to me reveals a heart of trust. Never underestimate the power of one surrendered glance. It moves my heart. One glance with the desire to draw near to me will cause me to draw near to you. Look to me. I can read the concerns and questions in your eyes. I can see your fear, your disappointment, and frustrations. Take heart. I can handle them. Where you are full of fear, I want to give you cause to smile. Where you are frustrated and disappointed, I want to fill you with joy. This joy is perfect and complete. It will protect you from despair and open your eyes to my goodness. It will cause you to see that I am at work and lead you into celebration. This kind of joy can only be found in me.

My joy will fuel you for my Kingdom and cause hope and energy to flow from your life. You believe in me. You talk about me. You worship me. You serve me. I love all that. Now, let me fill you with the life-giving energy of my Spirit so that your joy will be uncontainable. Then everything you think, do, and say will overflow with my joy. You will be an echo of my goodness and joy. My complete joy will be your experience day by day."

DECLARATION

I am an echo of my Father's joy. His life-giving Spirit fills me with joy, gives me strength, and is uncontainable. I carry His joy.

ACTIVATION

Ask Father God to fill you afresh with His life-giving Spirit so that your joy will be uncontainable. Intentionally look for ways to share your joy today and light up someone's life.

———

Psalm 27:13; Romans 15:13; James 4:8

DAY 15

'Sing, barren woman, you who never bore a child; burst into song, shout for joy, you who were never in labour; because more are the children of the desolate woman than of her who has a husband,' says the Lord.

— ISAIAH 54:1

"My message never changes. It remains the same. 'Sing. Sing. Sing.'

Regardless of the situation in which you find yourself, sing. Sing of my goodness. Sing of my glory. Sing of my splendour. Sing of my compassion. Sing of my protection. Sing of my provision. Sing of my power. Sing of my love. 'Sing. Sing. Sing.'

Do you find yourself in a season of barrenness? I am bigger than that. You honour me well by not fixing your eyes on what you can see, but by choosing to fix your eyes on who I am. I understand your pain. I see your grief. I hear your heart breaking. I am bigger than all that. As you find the strength to sing, you will experience my comfort. I am close to you and will nurse your broken heart. I will lift your head. You may feel crushed in spirit. I will save you. You may feel like a bruised reed. You won't break. You might feel the flame in your life is only just flickering. It won't go out. I am close to you. I have my eye on you.

Sing in your barrenness and watch the door of your life swing wide open to the best I have for you. As you sing, your 'Why me?' and 'Why is this happening?' will turn to 'What are you saying to me, Lord?' and 'What do you want to do in and through me because of what I am facing?' Sing, and you will see the good as I mould and shape you into the likeness of my Son. Sing, and your joy will be complete. Sing, and you will find the strength to stand."

DECLARATION

I know that my Redeemer lives and I have reason to sing and shout for joy. The one who gives me life will help me to keep standing until that day when He comes to take His stand here on earth.

ACTIVATION

Ask your Redeemer how He sees your situation and what song He is singing over you in the midst of it. Write it down. Stand on it. Strengthen yourself in the truth of His words: "You won't break. Your fire will not go out. I will lift your head and save you."

———

Job 19:25; Psalm 34:18; Isaiah 42:3; Matthew 12:20; Romans 8:28-29

DAY 16

When your words came, I ate them; they were my joy and my heart's delight, for I bear your name, Lord God Almighty.

— JEREMIAH 15:16

"You are my representative. You bear my name. Everything you do and say points to me. I love the way you bring honour to my name by loving me first and then others. Still, there is so much more I want to do in and through you. Your love for me and for others can go further and reach depths you don't know exist. Are you willing to let your circumstances take you to those depths? Are you willing to let me grip you by my power and do a work in and through you that is worthy of who I am? Can you trust me with all your heart like Mary did and say, 'I am the Lord's servant. I accept whatever he has for me'?

The only way you can go to those places of surrender and acceptance is by looking for my words. When you find a word from me, eat it. Chew on it. Let it become your joy and your heart's delight. You already know that my words are sweeter than honey and more precious than gold. You know that they nourish you. You need to know that my words will sustain you. As you eat my words they will nourish your very being and keep you from turning away and giving up on what I am doing in and through you. Sometimes, all the help you need from me is a word of truth. Find joy in my words and they will have the power to re-energise and refuel you with life and hope. My words will give you understanding, wisdom, and insight. Treasure them more than your daily food and your joy will be complete."

DECLARATION

The words my Father speaks to me are faithful and true. They lead me to a place of trust and joy.

ACTIVATION

Ask Father God how He wants you to represent Him today and do it with great joy. It is an honour and a privilege to be His hands and feet.

———

Job 23:12; Psalm 19:10; 119:103; Luke 1:38; 2 Corinthians 5:20

DAY 17

I have loved you with an everlasting love; I have drawn you with unfailing kindness. I will build you up again, and you *(put in your own name)* will be rebuilt. Again you will take up your timbrels and go out to dance with the joyful.

— JEREMIAH 31:3-4

"Nothing you have experienced in life is greater and more powerful than my everlasting love. No force can hold you back from being drawn in by my unfailing kindness. Nothing compares to my everlasting love and unfailing kindness. Allow this kind of love and kindness to flood your life and watch the miracle of restoration. Fragments will become whole again because my heart is to rebuild. Remember, in my Kingdom nothing is wasted. If I can take dust and breathe life into it, then I can take the rubble of your life and reshape it into something beautiful. My heart is to restore. I will restore everything that has been taken from you. My heart is to redeem. I will redeem the things that seem lost. Trust my love and kindness and you will find yourself dancing with the joyful again. Sorrow may have been your experience for a season but joy always comes in the morning. I am faithful and my mercies are new every morning. There is no reason to despair.

My love and kindness are wooing you into my presence - the place of redemption, restoration, rebuilding, and reshaping. That is where you will find deep, authentic, and real joy. Sorrow needn't become your identity. Choose joy. Let joy become a way of life. Step into my presence and experience complete joy."

DECLARATION

I dance for joy because my Father has loved me with an everlasting love. He has drawn me into His presence with His unfailing kindness. He is restoring and rebuilding my life. I can trust Him.

ACTIVATION

Ask Father God what He wants to do in you today. Give Him permission to have His way.

———

Psalm 16:8; Lamentations 3:17-24

DAY 18

Though the fig tree does not bud and there are no grapes on the vines, though the olive crop fails and the fields produce no food, though there are no sheep in the pen and no cattle in the stalls, yet I will rejoice in the Lord, I will be joyful in God my Saviour. The Sovereign Lord is my strength; he makes my feet like the feet of a deer, he enables me to tread on the heights.

— HABAKKUK 3:17-19

"Look at Habakkuk's life and learn the power of choosing joy. His name means 'he that embraces; wrestler'. Every time he heard it he was reminded that he would be one who wouldn't give in to circumstances. He would embrace them, but as a wrestler. They would not defeat him. The confession Habakkuk makes here is one of the greatest confessions of faith. Habakkuk was faced with his nation being invaded by a merciless enemy. He knew that many of his people would be dragged into exile and his land would be ruined; the temple destroyed. Rather than running and hiding and letting fear take over, he came to me and acknowledged his trust in me. You can do the same.

I am always here. Come to me and face your doubts and questions in my presence. When you face them in the presence of fear, confusion and doubt will confront you. In my presence, you will find strength, joy, and peace showing you a way forward. Declare your trust in me. Rejoice in me and strength will become your companion. Embracing joy, even in the midst of loss, pain, grief, frustration, and confusion, will strengthen your legs and you will be able to stand no matter what is thrown at you. Thank me that even though things may not be going the way you had hoped today, you have the opportunity to strengthen some spiritual muscles, which haven't been used in a very long time. I want to show you a different aspect to faith. There is faith that can see circumstances completely changed but there's also another kind of faith. Faith that sees you changed to face the circumstances with confidence, peace, and joy. Remember, I always take notice of you. My aim is to make you like my Son. Everything in your life, when surrendered to me with rejoicing, is used to do just that. Rejoice and let faith arise, to change you so that circumstances no longer defeat you. Then your joy will be complete."

DECLARATION

I may not see the breakthrough I am looking for, but I choose to rejoice in my Father. I will be joyful in the one who saves me and enables me to believe even though I can't see any results yet. I will be joyful in the one who steadies my feet and enables me to keep on going, even though it is tough.

ACTIVATION

Ask Father God for three truths that you can rejoice in and hold onto as you walk through today. Write them down.

———

Psalm 97:12; Habakkuk 3:17-19; Luke 1:47

DAY 19

At that time Jesus, full of joy through the Holy Spirit, said...

— LUKE 10:21

"At times you may wonder where your joy has gone. That's the time not to give in to how you are feeling, lest you get stuck and it becomes a way of life. Instead, ask me to fill you with joy through the Holy Spirit. It delights my heart when my children come to me and ask for the things they need. My Son did it all the time. I invite you to do the same. If my Son needed to be filled with joy through the Holy Spirit, then how much more do you?

There is no shame in asking. Remember, 'Ask and you will receive.' Do you need joy today? Ask! I will give it to you. Ask and keep asking! Once you have received joy, give thanks, and start sharing it with others. Let my joy bubble up in you. Let it become a gurgling brook leaking life and joy everywhere it flows. Dry places will come alive again. As you give away what you have received, you will receive even more. My Kingdom is very different to the world's kingdom. In the world's kingdom, you accumulate to become rich. In my Kingdom, you give away and become rich. Give what I have given to you and you receive even more, pressed down, shaken together, and running over.

It's not just about receiving joy but also giving it away. Always be generous with the things I give you and your joy will be a watering hole for many. Give your life of joy for my glory and you will receive it back with bonus and blessing. You will experience my complete joy."

DECLARATION

The joy of the Lord is welling up inside me. I will release it everywhere I go. I have freely received. Therefore I give freely.

ACTIVATION

Ask the Lord for His joy today. Intentionally, turn any sad or anxious thoughts into happy, thankful thoughts. At the end of the day, take stock as to how this impacted things for you.

———

Matthew 7:7; Luke 6:38; 10:21

DAY 20

I have told you this so that my joy may be in you and that your joy may be complete.

— JOHN 15:11

"Oh, wouldn't you love the joy you have to be complete, whole, and perfect for where you are, for who you are, for what you're facing, and for what you're doing? The only way you will experience complete joy is by allowing the joy of my Son to consume every area of your life.

I loved my Son before the foundations of the world and I love you with that same love. My Son learned to let my love nourish His heart. He walked in obedience because of my love for Him. He found satisfaction in fulfilling my purpose for His life. My love gave Him everything He needed. He learned to be at home in my love and His joy was complete.

It is possible for your joy to be complete and to overflow in every area of your life. Many things will vie for your attention. They will want to take the place of my joy. The only way you can guard the joy that is yours is by learning to be at home in my love for you. That is the key. When you know without a shadow of doubt that I love you and that I want the best for you, then walking in my ways will be your joy. Surrender and obedience will become your companions. You will know the meaning of true freedom and the privilege of receiving grace day by day.

Only as you walk in what I supply, will you know true and authentic joy. It will run deep in you and be complete. It will become a fountain that overflows to those around you."

DECLARATION

I am at home in my Father's love for me. His love nourishes me. His love gives me confidence that His plans for me are for good.

ACTIVATION

Ask the Father to reveal His love to you. Ask Him how He sees you. Ask Him how you can become more at home in His love. Receive what He says and walk in it.

———

John 15

Be joyful in hope, patient in affliction, faithful in prayer.

— ROMANS 12:12

"Being joyful isn't something you do when you feel like it. It is actually a command of mine. My desire and heart for you is that you are always full of my joy. I can already hear your response, 'But, how? That's impossible.'

Remember, my grace is always there for you and there is always enough of it to see you through each command I give you. I never give you a task and then leave you on your own to follow it. My grace is always enabling and empowering you, if you are willing to draw on it and make use of it. Grace is my divine influence in your life.

There is nothing that gives me greater pleasure than to see my children be joyful in hope, patient in affliction, and faithful in prayer. The only way you will be faithful in prayer, is if you are patient in the hard times. And the only way you will be patient in the hard times, is if you are joyful in hope.

Your joy has to be rooted in something so that it can multiply. The best soil for it to grow in is my life, my grace, and the hope you have of sharing in my glory. You have been made right in my sight because of your faith in my Son. Jesus has brought you into a place of undeserved privilege. It's a place of complete peace, that exceeds anything the world can offer. This is the source of your joy. It is secure. You can have confidence in it. It will enable you to be patient when trouble hits so that you will keep on praying and not give up on all that I have for you.

Focus on me. Make a big deal about who I am. Magnify me in every situation you face. I am bigger and greater than the deepest pit in which you may find yourself. I am bigger and greater than the highest mountain you need to climb. I am bigger and greater than the toughest impossibility you are facing at the moment. Faith doesn't wait for the pit, or the mountain, or impossibility to disappear before it can live out joy. Faith praises me and declares my word to be true, putting joy into practice until you've overcome. You will find yourself walking in complete joy."

DECLARATION

I will not be defeated by what I am experiencing. God has made me an overcomer. With my praise I overcome. My joy is rooted in who God says He is. He is greater and bigger than any problem or impossibility I am facing. I will rejoice in my Lord, magnifying who He is, and sing His praise for all to hear.

ACTIVATION

Look at that pit, mountain, or impossibility in front of you and start magnifying your Lord. Declare truth over that situation which seems too hard to handle. Take a moment to laugh at the impossibility and declare that your God is greater and bigger.

Romans 5:2-3; Philippians 4:4; 1 Thessalonians 1:6

DAY 22

You have loved righteousness and hated wickedness; therefore God, your God, has set you above your companions by anointing you with the oil of joy.

— HEBREWS 1:9

"I love to anoint my people with the oil of joy. When you love what I love and hate what I hate, you become qualified for my oil of joy. My oil of joy keeps you rooted. It strengthens you. It refreshes you. It brings healing to your mind, emotions, and body. Remember, a cheerful heart is good medicine.

My oil of joy will give you a cheerful heart. It will save you from a broken spirit sapping strength and energy. My oil of joy will enable you to shine. You will glow. You will radiate. You will carry me everywhere you go. You will naturally be salt and light in a flavourless and dark world.

My oil of joy is your protection. It protects your heart from disappointment, discouragement, and depression. It keeps you from holding on to unforgiveness, grudges, and bitterness. My oil of joy helps you to see others with my eyes and to listen to them with my ears. My oil of joy will make your joy complete."

DECLARATION

God has anointed me with the oil of joy. His oil of joy brings healing to my mind, emotions, body, and soul, so that I can be a blessing to others. A cheerful heart is good medicine. Joy is a choice and I choose joy today.

ACTIVATION

Search your heart. Is there any disappointment, discouragement, unforgiveness, or bitterness you need to surrender? Receive the oil of joy and imagine it being applied to those wounded areas bringing healing and joy. Thank God for His healing.

———

Proverbs 15:13; 17:22

DAY 23

For what is our hope, our joy, or the crown in which we will glory in the presence of our Lord Jesus when he comes? Is it not you? Indeed, you are our glory and joy.

— 1 THESSALONIANS 2:19-20

"When your joy becomes rooted in me, you will begin to see the bigger picture I have for you. Learning to live in my joy will equip you not only to thrive in your own circumstances but also to see my other children with pride and joy. They will benefit from the pride and joy you have for them. Jesus was able to endure all the pain and shame of the cross because He knew the joy that was waiting for Him, the glory that would follow his suffering. What was His joy? You. You are His pride and joy. He knew that His suffering wasn't in vain but that you and many others would be the ones to benefit from it.

Being rooted in my joy will give you a love for others and a desire to see them thrive and go on for me. I have made each one of you uniquely. You are individuals. But I never designed you to live independently. You need me and you need one another. My joy will help you to support one another. My joy will qualify you to hold up the arms of others who are flagging. The simple act of being there for one another, wanting the best for each other, and genuinely rejoicing with one another will cause your joy to go from strength to strength.

You need me. You need one another. Sometimes, you are there to carry the burdens of another. Other times, they are there to carry your burdens. This is real joy, community done well. Doing life with me prepares you to do life with others. Love me with all your heart, soul, mind, and strength and love others as I have loved you. Just as your love for me brings me great joy, so will your love for others will bring them and yourself great joy. You will know a joy over and above anything you have ever experienced."

DECLARATION

I am my Father's pride and joy. Jesus endured the cross because I was His joy. I am forgiven. I am free. I live the full life in Christ. I rejoice in that and nothing can take that away from me.

ACTIVATION

Ask God for someone you can celebrate and honour today. Once you've got the name of someone, ask God how you should show that person that they are a joy.

———

Galatians 6:2; Philippians 1:7; 2 Timothy 1:4; Hebrews 12:2; 2 John 1:12

DAY 24

Though you have not seen him, you love him; and even though you do not see him now, you believe in him and are filled with an inexpressible and glorious joy.

— 1 PETER 1:8

"There is nothing that pleases my heart more, and causes my joy to be released, than to see you love and trust me wholeheartedly even though you have never seen me. This is what I call faith and it is precious to me. Remember, without faith, you cannot please me. I know it can be hard to keep going when you can't see me, let alone what I am doing. But I can give you the grace to believe and to not give up. Just ask me.

With every choice to love and trust me no matter what, I will give you a joy that you won't be able to put into words. It's a joy that has a hint of the glories of Heaven. It's a joy that sees Heaven touch the ordinary and mundane and bring life. It's a foretaste of what is to come. Your love for me and your trust in me release joy. This kind of joy leads to life, a full life, life as I intended for you. It leads to salvation, the gift Jesus brought to the world we created.

I bless you for believing in me even though you have never seen me. There is perfect joy when you live by faith and not by sight. You have no reason to droop your head or drag your feet. Lift your head and pick up your feet. Keep believing for what you do not yet see and you will find the strength to thrive in life's cramped conditions. You will find complete joy."

DECLARATION

I choose to love and trust my Father, no matter what. I have the grace to lift my head, pick up my feet, and be part of Heaven touching earth because of the joy I carry.

ACTIVATION

Are there any areas in your life where you are dragging your feet? Surrender them to the Father. Thank Him for grace to believe. Thank Him for strength to thrive. Thank Him for joy to overcome. Thank Him that no cramped condition in your life will thwart His purposes for you.

———

John 10:10; 20:29; 2 Corinthians 5:7

DAY 25

We write this to make our joy complete.

— 1 JOHN 1:4

"John writes as an eye-witness of my Son, Jesus. He was there. He saw Jesus in the flesh. He listened to His words of life. My Son was the Word of life made flesh. The Word that came alive to the disciples is the same Word that can come alive to you. His life always was. He existed with me before the beginning of time and became visible to mankind to bring hope and joy.

Your joy is made complete when you embrace this life. When His life becomes your life, you will be full of joy. You will want to share it with everyone around you. Every time you share this good news, your joy will increase. My desire from the beginning of time was to be in relationship with you, my created loved one. The more we become one, the more you have to give to others around you.

Remember my commandment: love me with all your heart, mind, soul, and strength and love your neighbour as yourself. The more you love me, the more you can love your neighbour.

The more you love your neighbour, the more you will love me. This is the cycle of joy. This is where you experience complete joy. No one can rob you of this joy, only if you allow it to happen. Your joy in me is always secure. Be stubborn and don't let anyone take my joy away from you so that your joy will be complete."

DECLARATION

In Christ, my joy is complete. I choose to enter the cycle of joy today by loving my Father with all my heart, mind, soul, and strength and loving others the way Jesus loves me.

ACTIVATION

Is there someone in your life you find hard to love? Start to pray for him/her. Ask God for a supernatural love for that person. Spend some time enjoying God's presence and His love, which is surrounding you now.

———

John 16:22-24

DAY 26

I have no greater joy than to hear that my children are walking in the truth.

— 3 JOHN 1:4

"John has captured my heart here. His heart beat with the same heartbeat that I have for people. When I see you walking in the light and in truth, it fills me with great joy. There is no greater pleasure as a Father than to see you whole and walking in everything I have for you. My light and truth have to be your guide. They not only pave the way for your own life but they are building blocks for good and healthy relationships. Jesus is your light. When you follow Him, you won't walk in darkness. When you are in His light, your eyes will be opened to the truth, and you will be able to live in fellowship, true community, with those around you.

Nothing undermines fellowship more than pretense and dishonesty. You don't need to be what you are not. Be who I made you to be and walk in my light and truth. Your security is in me, not in what others say or think. Don't be afraid to show that you are a beautiful work in progress, still growing, changing and being moulded by hands of love. Be real. Be authentic. Be genuine. Be true. Walk in the light I give you. You will give others freedom to be themselves and open the door for them to walk in the light and truth, as well. Live according to my standards. Take the high road. Be the magnet that draws others into my ways. You will experience a joy like you have never known before, a joy that is whole and complete."

DECLARATION

God gives me boundaries and guidelines for my own protection. Following His commandments bring me great joy. They are not burdensome. They make my joy complete.

ACTIVATION

Ask Father God if there is any area of darkness in your life. Repent and renounce it. Ask Him what walking in the light looks like for you. Write it down and put it into practice.

———

John 8:12; 1 John 1:7; 3 John 3

DAY 27

To him who is able to keep you from stumbling and to present you before his glorious presence without fault and with great joy - to the only God our Saviour be glory, majesty, power and authority, through Jesus Christ our Lord, before all ages, now and forevermore! Amen.

— JUDE 1:24-25

"I am the one who keeps you from stumbling. I am the one who gives you the power and the desire to do what pleases me. Have complete confidence in my ability to protect and guard you. You are safe in my love. My love will never fail you. I am the one who makes you strong. Look to me as you run the race of life and you will finish well. Because of Jesus, you have the privilege and honour of being in my presence without fault and with great joy. Walk in that privilege.

There is no room for shame, guilt, or regret in my glorious presence. You are free. Walk freely into all that I have for you. I am your God and Saviour. I am your peace. I am your joy. I am your stronghold. In me your will find nothing broken and nothing missing. Step into who I am and I will become your reality.

I am the one who makes you holy and keeps you blameless until my Son, Jesus, comes back again. If I have said that I will do it, then I will do it. You can trust my word because I, who have called you my own, am faithful and I will make it happen. All glory, majesty, power, and authority belong to me. There is no one greater than I. You will find no one like me. You are safe in my hands. Your joy will be made complete in me."

DECLARATION

Because of Jesus, I am presented before my Father without fault and with great joy. He is the one who keeps me from stumbling.

ACTIVATION

Are you carrying shame, regret, or guilt? If so, lay them down. Keep reminding yourself today that Father God sees you as pure, holy and blameless because of Jesus.

———

Romans 16:25; 1 Thessalonians 5:23-24; Jude 1:21

DAY 28

Let the heavens rejoice, let the earth be glad; let them say among the nations, 'The Lord reigns'.

— 1 CHRONICLES 16:31

"You have reason to rejoice. You have reason to be happy. You have reason to live. I reign. I am in control. I am the one who has created all things and have put everything in place. I have placed you where you are and nothing can move you from my purposes for your life. The only one who can thwart my plans for your life is you. Give me your 'yes' and watch what I can do with your surrendered heart. When you seek me with all that you are, you will find reason to rejoice.

Glory in my name. Give thanks to me. Declare my greatness. Sing to me. Exalt me in your life. Always look for me and rely on my strength instead of your own. Never forget the wonders I have performed in your life. Remember the miracles. If I did it once, I can do it again.

I am the Lord your God who reigns in power. Rejoice in me. Remember the promises I have made and given to you. They can never be broken. You are secure because of each and every one of them. When these truths become realities in your life, not only do you acknowledge that I am in control but you also bring glory to my name. Others see that glory and are drawn to me because of you. Rejoice. Be glad. Your life has purpose. Embrace these truths and your joy will be complete."

DECLARATION

My God reigns. Hallelujah! My God reigns. Nothing will take Him by surprise or knock Him off His throne. He reigns and He is in control of everything I face today. I can trust Him completely.

ACTIVATION

Ask God if there are any areas in your life where you are finding it hard to trust Him. Surrender. Give Him your fears. Receive His love. Receive His power. Receive His spirit of self-discipline. Thank Him for His gifts.

———

1 Chronicles 16:8-15

DAY 29

Do not rejoice that the spirits submit to you, but rejoice that your names are written in heaven.

— LUKE 10:20

"Where is your joy rooted? In what do you triumph? Do you rejoice because you have authority over evil? Is your joy dependent on what you do for me? If so, you will experience disappointment.

Rejoice that I have authority over your life and have got you safe in my hands. Rejoice that no one can snatch you from me. Rejoice that my presence is always with you. I will never leave you to struggle on your own. I will always give you what you need for every situation you face.

Rejoice in what I have done for you through my Son, Jesus. He came as one of you and was perfectly God. He died as you, rose again, and closed the gaping hole between you and me, once and for all.

We can now walk in harmony because of what Jesus did. He satisfied every requirement for your wrong so that now I can look on you and see perfection. This is reason to triumph and rejoice.

The only reason you have authority is because I have given it to you. It's my power at work in you that enables you to please me and do the works I have planned for you. Find your reason for joy in me, and you will live a life of complete joy."

DECLARATION

My joy is found in the finished work of Jesus Christ. Because of Him I can walk in complete harmony with my Father. Christ is my reason for joy.

ACTIVATION

Take some time to rejoice in the finished work of Jesus and the power you have because of the cross. Ask Father God to give you a fresh appreciation for what Jesus did for you. Write a prayer of praise and thanksgiving.

———

John 10:28-29

DAY 30

In that day they will say, 'Surely this is our God; we trusted in him, and he saved us. This is the Lord, we trusted in him; let us rejoice and be glad in his salvation...' You will go out in joy and be led forth in peace...

— ISAIAH 25:9; ISAIAH 55:12

"Your greatest joy is my salvation. My salvation is complete. It is perfect. It is what the world needs. I am waiting for those I have created to come to me so that I can show them my love and compassion. I have put eternity in the hearts of everyone created in my image. Eternity is a deep longing for what is not yet. It's a realisation that there is more and the ability to live in the now with your eyes on what is to come. Eternity is a revelation of the bigger picture I have for my loved ones and the world in which they live. And it is an invitation to be part of what I am doing to see my purposes prevail.

Rejoice because of salvation, sin no longer has a hold on you. Rejoice that you are no longer defined by death but by life. Rejoice because you are my holy temple. You are clean and pure in my eyes. Rejoice that I am alive in you and my Spirit lives in you. Rejoice that I am your King. Rejoice that you carry my glory and my presence and the good work I have started in you, I will finish. Rejoice that you don't need to do life in your own strength. Rejoice because power and grace are your companions in life.

I am the God of peace. I am the one who leads you and guides you. I am the one who makes a way for you. I am the one who satisfies your soul. Let me saturate you with my living water and the oil of my joy. Let me breathe on your life and revive you with my joy. I am the one who holds you. I am your greatest support. I will never push you away or leave you. Embrace these truths and you will go out in joy. My peace will be made whole. Your joy will be complete."

DECLARATION

I rejoice in my salvation. Sin no longer has power over me. God gives me the power to say 'no' to sin and 'yes' to Him. With every 'yes', I experience more of His joy. He satisfies me completely and nourishes my soul with His breath of life and living water. I am alive in Him and I will go out with joy.

ACTIVATION

Spend some time quietly in your Father's presence and let Him breathe on you and nourish you with His living water and oil of joy. (Play some worship music, if you like)

———

Isaiah 30:18; 49:10; 51:3-5

DAY 31

Hallelujah! For our Lord God Almighty reigns. Let us rejoice and be glad and give him glory! For the wedding of the Lamb has come, and his bride has made herself ready. Fine linen, bright and clean, was given her to wear.

— REVELATION 19:6-8

"Live with a spirit of joy. My Son is coming back for His bride. He is coming back for a pure bride. You are His bride and He is coming back for you. Life, as you know it now, is preparing you for that triumphant day when you will see Him in all His glory. You are being refined and purified so that you will be one of those dressed in fine linen, bright and clean. Learn to celebrate now. Learn to rejoice now. You can celebrate me. You can rejoice in me. One day, your celebration and rejoicing will be complete as you stand in my presence and are able to share in my Son's glory because of the way you lived life here in the now.

It'll all be worth it. It'll all make sense. It'll all become clear. What has been hidden will be revealed. You will be presented as the beautiful bride, the wife of the Lamb. What a day that will be. Rejoice in anticipation. Let this truth and revelation motivate you to make the most of the life we have together here on earth. Live with a deep consciousness of who I am. Trust me. Know that you have a future with me. Life isn't just about the things you can see now. It's also about the treasures you are laying up for the future. Seek my Kingdom. That is the only Kingdom worth your living and investment."

DECLARATION

My life today is preparing me for what is yet to come. Nothing is wasted. I choose to live every moment for the glory of my bridegroom and look forward to being presented as His pure and perfect bride. What an honour and privilege. I align myself with Him, seeking first His Kingdom as that is the only Kingdom worth my time.

ACTIVATION

Ask the Father how you can make yourself ready for this glorious day and do what He says.

———

Matthew 6:33; 1 Peter 1:17-25; Revelation 21:2, 9

EPILOGUE

M aybe you have come to the end of this booklet and you have realised that you don't have a real relationship with God as your Father, Friend, Saviour, and Guide. He seems distant and you have been trying to live a good life in your own strength. If so, I'd love to lead you in a prayer. It's a prayer that will open the door of your life to the full life Jesus came to give you.

Father God, thank you for sending Jesus. Jesus, thank you for dying on the cross for me. I believe that you died for me personally and I declare that you are Lord. I choose to surrender myself, my pride, all my self-made plans and striving to be something I'm not, to cover up who I really am, and my rejection of who you are. I renounce partnering with a life-style that was not your intention for me. I repent and turn away from that mindset. And now I choose to embrace life with you through the death and resurrection of Jesus and the power of the Holy Spirit. Fill me with yourself and your Spirit. Fill me with love, power, self-discipline, joy, and peace. Thank you that you have taken all my shame and guilt and you now see me as righteous and perfect because of Jesus' blood shed on the cross for me. Thank you for forgiveness. Thank you for freedom. Thank you for the full life I have in Christ. I choose to embrace it and walk in it for your honour and glory.

In Jesus' name, Amen.

You have now started a life-changing journey with Father God. I want to encourage you to find other people on this journey and start to do life together. Let God continue to speak to you and guide you.

———

I would love to hear from you. Contact me at kingdombreakthrough.org

ABOUT THE AUTHOR

 Paige Squirrell is a writer, coach and leader. She has a passion to see God's Presence released in the lives of ordinary people bringing them to a place of real freedom. Paige longs to see people adopt a meaningful Kingdom lifestyle that brings joy and peace. Together with her husband Jonathan she co-leads Kingdom Breakthrough Ministries: equipping and releasing God's people everywhere.

She loves being a wife and has found real joy in raising four children. She recently became a grandmother and enjoys every minute of it.

Paige is a licensed minister of The Apostolic Network of Global Awakening and a regional consultant for the Filling Station Trust in East Anglia and London, UK.

facebook.com/kingdombreakthroughministries

FURTHER READING

ALSO BY PAIGE SQUIRRELL

Whispers from Heaven

Captivated by His Beauty

WITH JONATHAN SQUIRRELL

Thrive

Printed by Amazon Italia Logistica S.r.l.
Torrazza Piemonte (TO), Italy